Beginner's Guide to

★AMERICAN
TAE KWON DO

— by —

Keith D. Yates

President of
A-KaTo

American Karate And
Tae Kwon Do Organization
Garland, Texas

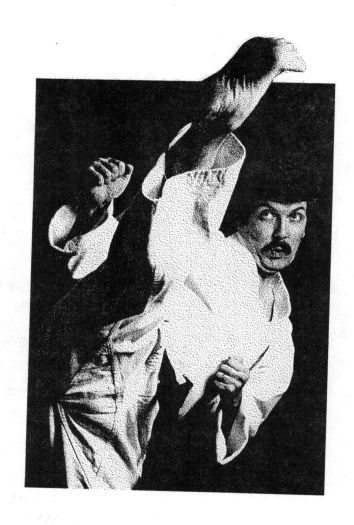

—Acknowledgements—

For my many students who
posed for and provided photos, thanks.

Appreciation also to Dr. Buddy Matthews
who gave his expert editorial help.

INTRODUCTION

American Tae Kwon Do came into its own during the late 1960s and early 70s. The art had been in this country for barely a dozen years when Americans began to turn it into a unique blend of traditions, practical self-defense and modern sport. American Tae Kwon Do is not so much a style of martial arts as much as a way of approaching the martial arts.

I want to mention something about the differences between Karate and Tae Kwon Do. As most Americans do it—there isn't much. *Karate* has become a generic term indicating any type of striking martial art. That is why many American Tae Kwon Do stylists, me included, use the terms Karate and Tae Kwon Do interchangably. You still see Koreans, even today, putting the word karate on the windows of their Tae Kwon Do schools.

Actually, you will find that the greatest difference between styles in America is whether or not they are "traditional" or "modern." There is confusion about these terms as well. The way I use them is: *traditional* Tae Kwon Do puts the emphasis on self-defense and on character-building aspects like discipline and respect. *Modern* or *sport* Tae Kwon Do places a much greater emphasis on tournaments and competition.

continued

Of course that is not to say that traditional schools never enter tournaments or that schools with a bunch of trophies in the window don't teach character-building, but you should check out the priorities of any school you want to train at and decide which is best for you.

The **American Karate and Tae Kwon Do Organization** is a "traditional" organization featuring by-and-large "Americanized" schools. We strongly believe in teaching the life-time benefits of the martial arts while incorporating elements from several disciplines that our instructors have found to be effective.

This book is a Manual for our style of American Tae Kwon Do known as **Nam Seo Kwan**, which literally means "School of the Southwest." I have written another book called the *Handbook of American Karate* which greatly expands the material you'll find in these pages. For a complete picture of American Karate you should get that book as well.

If you have any questions about our organization or about American Tae Kwon Do Nam Seo Kwan, please feel free to write me.

—*Keith D. Yates*
President A-KaTo
Founder, American Tae Kwon Do Nam Seo Kwan

A-KaTo
1218 Cardigan St.
Garland, TX 75040

CONTENTS

CHAPTER ONE **HISTORY** 7

CHAPTER TWO **PHILOSPHY** 19

CHAPTER THREE **THE CLASSROOM** 21

CHAPTER FOUR **TECHNIQUES** 35

CHAPTER FIVE **FORMS** 59

CHAPTER SIX **SPARRING** 73

CHAPTER SEVEN **SELF-DEFENSE** 89

CHAPTER EIGHT **GLOSSARY** 99

APPENDICES 103

少林弓影破反光源
九年生义不動丹·砣

李屋艾释贺

This picture is taken
from an old drawing
of **Bodhidharma**
who is,
according to
legend, the
father
of the
martial
arts.

*TEACHER'S NOTE: Bold face words in this chapter are
included on the test on martial arts history on page 16.*

CHAPTER ONE
HISTORY

The martial arts started in Asia, but no one is sure exactly how or even how long ago. There are many, many old stories about the various martial arts. One popular legend tells of a Buddhist monk named **Bodhidharma** who is said to have traveled to China from his native India about **525 A.D.**

He ended up at the Shaolin Monastery, where he found the monks weak and out of shape. The story tells how he taught them exercises that eventually became known as **Kung Fu**. Traveling monks introduced these exercises into other countries, including Okinawa, Japan and Korea, where they evolved into other systems.

OKINAWA and JAPAN

Okinawa is actually one of a group of little islands off the coast of Japan. Karate (which means **"empty hand"**) was born here several centuries ago from the influence of those Kung Fu practicing monks.

Although the Okinawans weren't allowed to carry swords, the karate practitioners sometimes used farm tools as weapons to defend themselves. You probably recognize the **sai** and the **nunchaku** from karate movies.

Gichin Funakoshi was a karate teacher in Okinawa who went to Japan in 1922 to demonstrate his art. The Japanese people liked karate so much that it soon became more popular there than in Okinawa itself.

Today there are several kinds (or "styles") of both Okinawan and Japanese karate.

KOREA

Kung Fu also made its way into ancient Korea. There the martial arts went by names such as **Subak** and **TaeKyon**.

During ancient times there was a group of warriors called the **Hwa-Rang**. Besides being soilders they had a code of conduct that taught them to be loyal, considerate, and brave.

In **1909** the Japanese Empire overran Korea and outlawed not only martial arts but also most Korean cultural practices. Many Koreans found

Figures from ancient Korean writitngs.

conditions at home so bad that they traveled to other countries, and some of them got to study other martial arts.

The end of World War II brought an end to the Japanese occupation. The Koreans were eager to get back to their own traditions and the martial arts were once again taught, this time with added influences from other countries.

Each **kwan** (school) had different methods of training. They used different names, including **Tang Soo Do** (the Korean translation of Karate*).

Many of the martial arts teachers in Korea wanted to gather the different schools under a single name. Finally, in **1955**, at a big meeting of instructors, they decided on **Tae Kwon Do** (which means "the way of kicking and punching"). The new name had been suggested by an army general, **Choi Hong Hi**.

The unification didn't last long, however. Soon General Choi took his organization (the International TKD Federation) out of Korea and the Koreans made up a new group: the World TKD Federation.

Today there are many different Tae Kwon Do organiza-

General Choi Hong Hi, who came up with the name Tae Kwon Do.

*Tang Soo Do means "way of the China hand" which was the orginal translation of Karate. G. Funakoshi changed the translation to "empty hand" to make the art more acceptable to the Japanese.

tions. The same thing is true of Karate and Kung Fu and just about all other martial arts. The martial arts do not have just one overseeing organization.

Actually, that isn't so bad because that way everybody can choose an organization compatible with what they want to acheive in the martial arts. Some groups like to stress nothing but self-defense. Others emphasize tournaments. And some, like the A-KaTo, practice both the sport and the self-defense aspects.

In Korea, Tae Kwon Do has changed a lot in the last 40 years. When the name was first created in 1955, the Korean system was very similar to Japanese karate. But the Koreans didn't want their style to be like other systems of karate. So

Ancient statues from Korea show what some people say are martial arts-like moves.

they increasingly began to emphasize kicking. They also wanted to get Tae Kwon Do into the Olympic Games, something karate had been trying to do unsuccessfully for years. Some Korean instructors didn't like the idea of making Tae Kwon Do into a sport and said that the style should only be taught as an art and as a means of self-defense. But when the Olympic Games were held in Korea in 1988 and Tae Kwon Do was introduced as a "demonstration" sport, even the critics seemed proud.

In the Olympic Games of the year 2000, Tae Kwon Do will join Judo as the only martial arts to be official Olympic sports. Unfortunately participants will be required to be members of the WTF.

The new "Olympic-style" Tae Kwon Do does not allow punches to the head or kicks to the groin. So most techniques are head-high kicks, instead of an equal mix of hands and feet that was common only a few years ago.

TAE KWON DO IN AMERICA

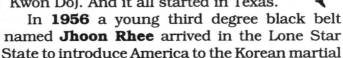

Experts say more than three-fourths of American martial artists practice Tae Kwon Do (or some version of Karate that came from Tae Kwon Do). And it all started in Texas.

In **1956** a young third degree black belt named **Jhoon Rhee** arrived in the Lone Star State to introduce America to the Korean martial arts. At the time Mr. Rhee, a student of the *Chung Do Kwan* school, taught *Tang Soo Do.*

This was during the time that the martial arts were undergoing great changes back in Korea. The name Tae Kwon Do was not in wide use and Tang Soo Do didn't mean anything to Westerners. So Mr. Rhee used the name *Karate* because it was more recognizable to Americans who had heard tales of "karate experts" told by returning service men from Japan and Okinawa after World War II.

Mr. Rhee soon started teaching at the University of Texas, and the first black belt out of that class would turn out to be one of the biggest pioneers of the martial arts in the United States. **Allen R. Steen** became known as "The Father of Texas Blood 'n Guts Karate" because of his chain of schools and his fierce reputation as a champion and trainer of champions.

A early photo of Jhoon Rhee demonstrating his power.

Steen opened the first karate school in Texas in 1962. In a few years he had established a chain of schools across in Texas. By then Mr. Rhee had moved to Washington D.C. and had started using the name Tae Kwon Do. But Mr. Steen and his followers in the Southwest continued to call their style Karate.

The same thing happened all across the USA in the late

Allen Steen demonstrates his famous flying side kick for FBI agents in the 60s.

50s and early 60s. Korean instructors arrived to make their fortunes in America and immediately began calling their style Karate. Their students became instructors themselves in a few years and "Korean Karate" became firmly established in the American lexicon.

American-born black belts were only interested in promoting Karate and Tae Kwon Do as effective fighting methods. They had no interest in the politics going on back in Korea between the various organizations. Many instructors, in fact, started their own organizations to promote the American approach.

The American style was indeed unique. During this early stage of American Karate and Tae Kwon Do, competition was rough! It was not uncommon for a competitor to get a broken nose or ribs and be expected to come back in the ring and dish out the same to his opponent. Needless to say, there weren't many kids involved in Tae Kwon Do in the 1960s.

In 1973, Jhoon Rhee introduced sparring pads, which allowed semi-contact without the risk of injury that had occured with bare-knuckled fighting. More competitors started entering tournaments in the mid to late 70s as sparring grew safer. American martial arts magazines featured stories on tournaments and on their champions.

Atheletic competition had been popular in America for a long time, and the tournament scene became the primary method for promoting Karate and Tae Kwon Do in this country. The American style came to be closely associated with a sporting approach. But the sport image soon stalled. Martial arts tournaments never became as big as football, boxing or even golf. To this day the only people in the stands at an American tournament are the families of the competitors.

Many of the sport karate heros themselves have ultimately found there is more to be gained, both personally and commercially, from turning back to an emphasis on the character-building

California's Chuck Norris(left) and Texan Skipper Mullins were two of the early heros of American martial arts tournaments in the 1960s.

aspects of martial arts. This is the A-KaTo's approach.

The winning 1970 Texas Karate Competition team consisted of Candy Simpson, Demetrius Havanas, Skipper Mullins and Keith Yates.

THE AMERICAN KARATE AND TAE KWON DO ORGANIZATION

Keith D. Yates as a seventeen year old first degree black belt in 1968.

In **1976** Keith D. Yates, one of Allen Steen's original black belts, formed the *Southwest Tae Kwon Do Association.* The Association grew steadily over the years, eventually including members in states outside of the Southwestern United States. On the Association's 20th Anniversary in 1996, Mr. Yates changed the name to the *American Karate and Tae Kwon Do Organization* to reflect not only the larger scope of the organization but also the change in Tae Kwon Do that had taken place over the previous two decades.

After years of trying, the Korean government finally got Tae Kwon Do included in the Olympic Games. Unfortunately, it is only members of the government-sponsored WTF organization who will be elligible to participate. Without getting into that controversy we *can* say that the general public is confused by the differences between the "old" traditional Tae Kwon Do and the "new" sport Olympic Tae Kwon Do.

The Olympic TKD training patterns have changed over the last 20 years (see the chapter on forms for more information). Their sparring rules are different. In fact, the whole emphasis has shifted dramatically towards a more "sporting" approach. The term Tae Kwon Do simply does not reflect the art as taught by most "traditional" American instructors anymore. That is many instructors, including Mr. Yates, have made a point of referring to their approach specifically as **"American Tae Kwon Do".**

But, alas, American Tae Kwon Do and American Karate have become overused terms these days. So many competitors in an open tournament say they are "Ameri-

13

Keith Yates charges an opponent at a early 1970s tournament.

can" stylists that the term has lost any meaning. Many so-called "American" stylists are talented martial artists—however some are not. In fact, to some, the term *American Tae Kwon Do* is an indication of a "watered-down" approach, even though that is usually not true.

So, several years ago, Mr. Yates came up with a "stylistic" name to go with the organization's approach—one that distinguishes it from the other American-style schools. **Nam Seo Kwan** (naam-sah-kwan) literally means **"School of the Southwest"** named after the original title of the association.

Today, not all schools within A-KaTo teach under the name *Nam Seo Kwan*, but the organization does require that they all maintain a *traditional* approach to their karate or Tae Kwon Do, keeping the "art" in the martial arts and with a bottom-line emphasis on self-defense.

This approach teaches basically the same system that Mr. Steen learned from Jhoon Rhee although many elements have been added and improved on by both Mr. Steen and Mr. Yates over the years.

For example, in the early 1980s Mr. Yates had the opportunity to begin training in ju-jutsu. He has incorporated many of that art's techniques into the advanced curriculum. Likewise, Kobudo (weapons techniques) is a part of A-KaTo's advanced training.

For the lower ranks *Nam Seo Kwan* uses the original Tae Kwon Do training patterns devised by the "Father of Tae Kwon Do," General Choi Hong Hi although we have never been affiliated with his organization (the ITF). At the higher levels we incorporate some of the old *Tang Soo Do* forms adapted from Mr. Rhee's original system.

A-KaTo also retains many traditions of the original Korean and Japanese systems. Low stances are emphasized rather than the modern

A-KaTo instructors in the early 1980s. Paul Hinkley, Bob Woerner, Keith Yates and Larry Wheeler.

upright "walking stances." There is a more equal mix of hand and foot strikes, as opposed to the 80% kicks of some newer schools of sport Tae Kwon Do. The head is a legitimate target for punches, and kicks to the groin are permitted as long as the student has proper control. Of course, complete respect and discipline are required.

Exact requirements for each lower rank are left to the individual A-KaTo instructor. All black belt testing is conducted under A-KaTo authority. This way, integrity and quality of instruction can be maintained within the organization and within *Tae Kwon Do Nam Seo Kwan.*

Although most of the A-KaTo instructors are Mr. Yates' own personally trained black belts the organization is open

to schools with other backgrounds. The A-KaTo does not, however, just accept anyone with an ability to fill out a form and mail it in. See page 105 for more info on membership in A-KaTo.

The A-KaTo does not claim that its system of Tae Kwon Do is superior to any other approach. Mr. Yates has always said that it is the *individual* rather than the *style* that makes a skilled martial artist. However within the framework of the A-KaTo many talented and dedicated martial artists will continue to develop. ■

Nam Seo Kwon founder, Keith Yates receives his 8th degree black belt from Allen Steen (left) and James Toney (right) in 1992.

QUESTIONS FROM CHAPTER ONE

Who was the Indian Buddhist monk who is said to have established martial arts-type exercises at the Shaolin Monastary in China?_____

Approximately what year was that? _____

What art did these exercises evolve into? _____

What does Karate mean? _____

What are a couple of Okinawan Karate weapons? _____

_____

Who took karate from Okinawa to Japan? _____

What are some of the names of ancient Korean martial arts?

_____

What was the name of the group of Korean warriors dedicated to loyalty and bravery? _____

When did Japan invade Korea? _____

When the United States liberated Korea many martial arts schools soon opened. What is the word for school ?_____

What is the Korean translation of karate?_____

What year did TKD get its name?_____

Who suggested it? _____

Who introduced the Korean martial arts to the U.S. and when?

_____

Who was the Father of Texas "Blood 'n Guts" Karate?

_____

What year was the Southwest TKD Assoc. (now the A-KaTo) founded?_____

Because the modern Korean approach has taken a turn towards the sporting aspect many instructors in the U.S. refer to their approach as_____ Tae Kwon Do.

What does Nam Seo Kwan mean? _____

Mr. Yates poses with the Father of American Tae Kwon Do, Grandmaster Jhoon Rhee, after a 6 A.M. workout (a regular routine for Mr. Rhee).

The Tenets of
AMERICAN
TAE KWON DO

태권도
신조

친절

겸손

고결

인내

자제

불굴의

정신

COURTESY

HUMILITY

INTEGRITY

PERSEVERANCE

SELF-CONTROL

INDOMITABLE
SPIRIT

CHAPTER TWO
PHILOSOPHY

One of the reasons people take up any martial art is the hope that they will learn more than simply how to defend themselves. They have heard that martial arts instill character-building aspects such as self-discipline, self-confidence, and respect for others.

No one would argue that these traits are needed in American society today. But are the martial arts a proper way to develop character? Can fighting techniques, of all things, really teach philosophy?

The answer is seen in hundreds of years and millions of practitioners. Yes, Karate, Tae Kwon Do, Kung Fu and the other martial arts can indeed teach a sense of discipline, honor and respect. They can, at least, if they are taught properly.

Traditionally taught, Tae Kwon Do stresses the development of the whole person. The mind and the character of the individual are just as important as the body.

> *"Martial arts without philosophy is merely street-fighting."*
>
> Jhoon Rhee

It has been said that there are three types of people in the world: those who make things happen, those who watch things happen, and those who don't know what is happening.

The key to becoming a leader who makes things happen is *self-confidence*, combined with the right *abilities*. Martial arts certainly teaches self-confidence. In addition, the self-discipline and focused learning attitude leads to the development of abilities not only in the Tae Kwon Do school but in everyday life. The modern "Tenets of Tae Kwon Do" reflect this attitude.

One of the most important concepts of the martial arts is that of respect for others. It is this principle more than any other that keeps the trained martial artist from using his or her skill in anything more than a legitimate self-defense situation.

The competent instructor teaches the students that they are responsible for their own actions. Tae Kwon Do ultimately results not only in the refinement of technique but in the advancement of mental control. A person who is in control is less likely to use their techniques to harm others.

This is what makes traditional Karate and Tae Kwon Do more than mere sports. Other sports may teach physical and mental discipline, but they don't necessarily teach respect and self-control—in fact, sometimes the opposite.

The story about the Olympic skater's willingness to do anything, even injure an opponent, to win shocks everyone. But isn't our society also at fault for placing so much emphasis on winning? Is being the best in any sport worth sacrificing our morals, our character, to that end?

Martial arts instructors everywhere proclaim the character aspects of the arts, yet many of them turn around and practically force their students into tournament competition and then wrongly encourage them to "go all out" to win. This defeats the very purpose of martial arts—striving to do your best but accepting whatever comes with strength and discipline of character.

An athlete trains all his or her life for a chance at the Olympics or for the "pros." One fall on the ice, one failed pass or kick can break a career. She can go from being a contender for the Gold Medal to fifth or sixth place. He goes from being the guy who could *win* the Super Bowl to the guy who *lost* the Super Bowl. Perhaps these pressures are to be expected in professional athletics, but they should not be forced upon the average martial arts student—especially young ones. Day to day effort is worth more in the dojang and in life than one super moment—especially when that one moment may never come!

There is a very real danger that if martial arts students can't be the best of the best, they may quit training altogether. Bruce Lee said that "in every passionate pursuit, the pursuit counts more than the object pursued." In other words, the *training* is more important than the *trophy*. As martial artists we should aim for excellence, but not for perfection. We should want to be OUR best, not necessarily THE best.

The Olympic Gold Medal, the Super Bowl Ring, the first place sparring trophy—all are worth striving for, but not worth sacrificing everything else for. The **pursuit** of excellence can be the reward in and of itself.

Confidence is the primary benefit of martial arts training. Life is a struggle and only in having the confidence to face the struggles can we grow and mature. ■

Two of the most important principles in Tae Kwon Do are **DISCIPLINE** and **RESPECT**. The first way a student learns these is through the formal bow.

In the attention posture (**Cha-ree-oh**) the student stands quietly at attention, not moving and only looking straight ahead. This takes longer for younger students to learn but it is an excellent way to develop discipline.

You must pay attention to learn.
You have to pay attention to the teacher.
This means you must have discipline.
Discipline means paying attention.

In Asian cultures bowing (**Kee-ung-yay**) is similar to shaking hands in America. But it is more than just a greeting, it is a show of respect toward the other person. Bow slowly to demonstrate that respect.

You have to respect your teacher. Not for his good but for your own good. If you respect the teacher you will learn more and you will learn faster. The instructor is also bowing to you. That shows that they respect you as well.

The student pledge of the American Karate And Tae Kwon Do Organization.

"HOW DO WE BUILD SELF-CONFIDENCE?"

"KNOWLEDGE in the Mind . . .

HONESTY in the Heart. . .

STRENGTH in the Body."

THE STUDENT PLEDGE

The instructor asks, **"How do we build self-confidence?"** Students then answer **"Through knowledge in the mind, honesty in the heart, and strength in the body."** (While pointing to head, then to chest, and then raising the fist.)

The instructor should make sure the students understand the meaning behind the pledge. The following is a good way to accomplish that.

"Self-confidence starts with **knowledge**. Knowledge is important. If you offer a monkey a banana or a diamond, which will he take? The banana, of course. The monkey doesn't know the diamond is more valuable. So knowledge teaches you what is valuable. I want you to concentrate just as much on school work as you do on your karate. If you can learn your karate techniques, you can learn your school lessons.

"But you cannot stop with knowledge. There are a lot of smart people that don't use their brains for good purposes. You must be a good person inside. You must have a good heart to use your knowledge. You must be **honest**. What is honesty? Not lying. Do people like you when you lie? Do you like yourself when you lie? So by being honest and by not lying, not only are you doing the right thing, but you will like yourself better and other people will also like you.

"The last thing is action. When you know the right thing to do, I want you to be able to do it. I want you to have the strength to do it. I want you to exercise every day. I want you to eat correctly every day. I want you to practice your Tae Kwon Do every day. When you have done all this your body will be **strong**."

This is the message of Tae Kwon Do. A true martial artist embodies a perfect balance of intellect, emotional character and strength.■

Author's note: I originally learned this pledge from Jhoon Rhee.

THE A-KaTo LOGO

The American Karate and Tae Kwon Do Organization logo consists of the yin/yan (Um/Yang in Korean) symbol set in a triangle.

The yin/yang is the ancient symbol of opposites. In the martial arts: it refers to the counter balancing aspects of hard and soft; empty hand and weapons techniques; kicks and punches, etc.

The triangle's three sides reflect the three aspects of martial arts training: the intellectual, the physical and the emotional (or mind, body, spirit). These three aspects are also reflected in our Student Pledge — "Knowledge in the mind, honesty in the heart, and strength in the body."

23

QUESTIONS FROM CHAPTER TWO

What are the "Tenets of Tae Kwon Do"?

_____

_____

_____

_____

_____

_____

What are the two principles taught in the bowing commands?

_____

What is the student pledge?

_____

_____

What is the ancient symbol of opposites?

_____

What are the three aspects of martial arts training as symbolized in the A-KaTo triangle?

_____

_____

_____

A teacher affects eternity; he can never tell where his influence stops.
—Henry Adams

"The martial arts should not be
considered a competitive sport.
One can be excellent in a certain game or
sport without necessarily
possessing an admirable character.
Being a good runner, boxer, wrestler
or swimmer does not mean being
a good person."

—Sang Kyu Shim

CHAPTER THREE

THE CLASSROOM

There are unwritten customs to be obeyed in the Tae Kwon Do class. Every student regardless of rank or seniority should be aware of and obey these rules. The traditions and manners of the martial arts not only set the mood but also help the beggining students learn and practice the principles of discipline and respect.

BOWING

Every class starts with bowing. The bow symbolizes respect for others as well as self-discipline (see page 21). There is no religious significance to the bow. In fact, the Asian bow is compared to the western handshake. The martial arts bow does, however, involve more than just a "greeting." You should bow to your teacher to show the respect he or she deserves because of their own dedication to karate and to you as their student.

UNIFORMS

The uniform all students wear is called a **tobak** (Korean) or often a **gi** (Japanese). Traditionally, they are white, but many American instructors allow uniforms in various colors. These loose-fitting, pajama-like outfits are well suited to vigorous physical activity. Besides, they help the student to feel like *real* martial artists.

Take care of your uniform. Keep it washed and pressed because how you keep up with your appearance is a reflection of how you feel about yourself.

BELTS

It is said that in ancient times the kimono belt of the advanced pratitioner would turn black with age and accumulation of dirt (the belt is never washed). Whether or not this is true, the black belt has become the accepted symbol of the stage at which the student becomes a teacher of others. Actually the wearing of colored belts is a modern innovation that most attribute to **Jigoro Kano**, who founded Judo in 1888.

AMERICAN TAE KWON DO

The wearing of colored belts to indicate rank has been a successful idea in modern martial arts, especially for Westerners, as American students like to have some sort of visible recognition of their acheivement.

Today there are many different belt colors which often vary from school to school (even within the A-KaTo). However, the student always starts out at white belt (a symbol of emptiness) and progresses through several stages until acheiving the black belt. Belt rank, by the way, is very important in the classroom. It is similar to military rank, with all the regulations and symbols of respect that you might suspect.

HOW TO TIE YOUR UNIFORM AND BELT

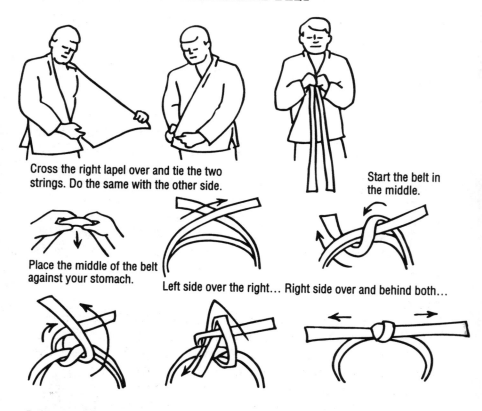

Cross the right lapel over and tie the two strings. Do the same with the other side.

Start the belt in the middle.

Place the middle of the belt against your stomach.

Left side over the right... Right side over and behind both...

Follow these drawing and when finished both ends of the belt should hang down the same length. (If there are stripes on your belt they should go on your left side.)

PROMOTIONS

Promotion to the next rank requires memorization and performance of techniques usually consisting of training patterns, kicks, self-defense demonstrations, sparring, and sometimes breaking boards. Criteria for promotion includes more than just physical techniques, however. Attendance and attitude are also critical, especially at the intermediate and advanced levels.

Most schools have time requirements for each belt level, although in some systems the student cannot test until the instructor tells grants permission (which can be months or even years).

Below are typical belt colors for the seven major categories of rank in a karate or Tae Kwon Do school.*

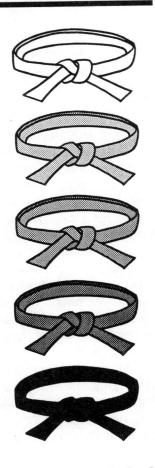

BEGINNING
   White
   Yellow
   Orange
INTERMEDIATE
   Purple
   Green
   Blue
ADVANCED
   Brown
   Red

BEGINING INSTRUCTOR
   1st Black
   2nd Black
ADVANCED INSTRUCTOR
   3rd Black
   4th Black
MASTER INSTUCTOR
   5th Black
   6th Black
   7th Black
GRANDMASTER INSTRUCTOR
   8th Black
   9th Black
   10th Black

* Not all schools have all these colored belts.
The WTF does not have a 10th dan, for example.

THE DOJANG (how to pick one)

The Japanese word **dojo** and the Korean word **dojang** both mean roughly *gymnasiaum* or *training hall*. Whatever you call your school, a clean and orderly environment is critical for a proper Tae Kwon Do class. But more important than the physical surroundings are the attitudes of the teacher and students. If you are looking for a school it is beneficial to speak with the instructors and with the students and parents of students to find out more about the school.

If you notice a bragadocious teacher, telling you all about his or her accomplishments instead of what you will be learning, that's a good sign that the instructor is not focused on the students.

Unfortunately there really are instructors like the "bad Sensei" in many karate movies. You want to find a teacher who cares about the students and who can communicate with them on a level they can understand (not all black belts can effectively teach children, for example).

Watch a class before you sign up. A good class reflects the attitudes previously discussed. Discipline must be obvious, but an extreme military-like atmosphere often stifes enjoyment. After all, Tae Kwon Do classes should be enjoyable or you won't want to come back.

Remember that maturity in the martial arts, or in life for that matter, is not acquired overnight. A good teacher will take time for his or her students.

That means making time for students' questions. In some very traditional classes students are never allowed to speak, let alone ask questions. Most Americans instructors, however will take the time to make sure everyone understands why they are doing a technique and how they should do it.

Americans are often impatient and want to learn more than they are ready for. A good teacher will not endulge the impatient student who is bored by the "same old thing," but will help his or her students overcome the bordem by refining the moves they already know.

PROCEDURES

When you enter the workout area for the first time be sure and bow in. You should also bow on your way out. Shoes should not be worn on the workout floor or mat.

At the command "one line," you should line up according to rank in ready position. The black belts also line up facing the students as shown below. The senior black belt is in the center of the line of students.

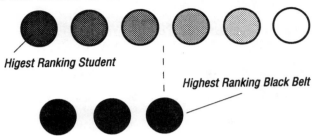

Higest Ranking Student

Highest Ranking Black Belt

The senior instructor will signal the highest ranking student who gives the formal bowing commands.

If you arrive late and miss the bow-in, stand at the edge of the mat and wait for the proper recognition and bow from a black belt instructor. If you need to leave for any reason, gain permission from a black belt.

If you want to ask a question, raise your hand and address the black belt by "Mr. Wheeler," "Mrs. Reeve," etc. After the answer you should respond with a bow. Also, bow if a black belt takes personal time during the drills to point out something to you.

The proper sitting position is cross-legged with the left leg (the non-aggressive side) covering the right. The back should remain erect. You should be quiet while sitting.

Before sparring, the students are to bow to the black belt and to each other. If a brown or red belt is conducting the sparring session, the students are to bow to each other but not to the brown or red belt. As you can see respect and protocal are very important in the classroom. Hopefully, this same attitude will carry over into other areas of the student's life.

31   AMERICAN TAE KWON DO

RULES OF THE CLASSROOM

Bow upon first entering and upon the last exit of the workout area.

Do not enter class late without acknowledgment of instructor (remain at the edge of the mat until the instructor bows you in). Note: Coming into class late shows a disrespect for others and penalty pushups may be assigned to those students.

If you arrive early—use the time to stretch and prepare for class. Running around playing is NOT preparation for class.

When called into formation—RUN. Lining up should not take more than 30 seconds.

Seek permission to leave class early (or to go to the restroom).

Be sure and bow out to the instructor if you are leaving class early.

Always address brown and black belts as "Sir," "Ma'am," "Mr.," etc. rather than "yeah" or "uh-huh."

Never pass between an instructor and the students as this is a sign of disrespect. Walk behind the other students instead.

Maintain eye-contact with the instructors when they are talking to you. In the attention position, or when being addressed by an instructor, do not let your attention wander to another group or activity.

When the instructor speaks to the entire group, ALL activity should stop.

After being directly addressed by a black belt, bow in acknowledgment.

Remain in Chunbi (ready position) between exercises.

Observe quietly and sit in proper position (legs crossed) while others spar.

Wear complete uniform in class.

Rough-housing is the opposite of courtesy and self-control.

Do not ask a black belt to spar. This is considered a sign of disrespect.

Do not ask to be promoted. This is a clear indication of wrong motives.

Even outside of class conduct yourself like a representative of the martial arts. For example, always show self-control and try to avoid fighting or showing-off.

Accept responsibility for your own actions. Do not let your ego control you.

A martial artist can only perform at peak efficiency by avoiding drugs and alcohol.

QUESTIONS FROM CHAPTER THREE

What is the Japanese name for the uniform?_____

What is the Korean name for the uniform?_____

Who invented the colored belt rank system?

_____

What are the seven categories of rank in American TKD?

_____

_____

_____

_____

_____

_____

_____

What are the Japanese and Korean words for gymnasium?

_____

After being addressed by a black belt the student should_____

WHAT'S WRONG
WITH THIS STATEMENT
"A HOOK KICK REALLY WORKS!"

All techniques work . . .

But on the other hand, all techniques fail . . .

. . . the point to remember is, you have to use the
technique in the proper situation, with the right
timing and with a certain type of opponent. So it
really isn't the "technique" that works it is "how" you
execute the technique that makes it work!
**Remember that
as you learn the techniques
in this chapter.**

CHAPTER FOUR
TECHNIQUES

Although martial arts stresses development of mind, body, and spirit, body is the area most people think of first. In this chapter you'll find a guide to the physical spects of American Tae Kwon Do training.

WARM UPS
Whether you are beginning a formal class or just working out at home, you should always start your physical activity with warm ups.

The very term "warm up" refers to the fact that during these initial exercises the body temperature actually rises. Blood flow increases through muscle tissue and the body begins to sweat. Warm ups make your muscles more pliable and more resistant to injury. These factors enable your body to perform at a higher level of efficency. A proper warm up not only helps to prevent muscle injury but reduces the chances of soreness afterwards as well.

STRETCHING
Stretching should be a part of any warm up period. Stretches increase your muscle flexibility. The word "muscle" comes from the Latin for mouse. Like a
mouse, the muscle has a tail (the tendon) that attaches to the bone. Muscles are the motors that move all the parts of your body. It's important to keep them flexible and strong.

Stretching is usually divided into two categories— **static**, or slow motions held for a period of time, and **ballistic**, or quicker bouncing motions.

While balistic stretches are often used in martial arts classes, static stretches are more easily controlled and are safer, especially for beginners.

AMERICAN TAE KWON DO

Here is a sitting-stretch routine. Hold each position for twenty to thirty seconds.

It is important that you keep your knees flat and your legs straight. As in all static stretches, you should not bounce up and down but just slowly pull and hold your position.

Finally reach out to each foot and pull yourself forward until your head touches the floor. Hold this for 20 seconds.

A stretching program must be performed more than once or twice a week to see results. Each time try to push yourself a little farther. The ideal however is a certain amount of discomfort, not pain. If you injure yourself by going too far it will mean you have to take time off from your training program to allow the muscle injury to heal.

Most people don't go to Tae Kwon Do class every day, but you can still stretch every day. You can even preform the sitting routine while you sit in front of the television. The important thing is to make stretching a habit. Otherwise you will never have those high kicks.

Two-person stretch:
Have your partner pull
you very slowly. It is
important to keep the
legs straight.

YOP ACHAOLLIGI
High side leg lift

AP CHAOLLIGI
High front leg lift

Swinging leg lifts (above) are often used in Tae Kwon Do classes. This is a **ballistic** stretch and should therefore be done with care. Be sure your muscles are already warmed up with slow stretches. Begin this exercise slowly being careful not to swing your leg up violently.

Situps should *not* be done by pulling the body all the way to a sitting position. Proper situps (usually called "crunches") should not go any farther than the pictures at right show. To attempt to sit all the way up actually works against the abdominal muscle group and can cause lower back soreness.

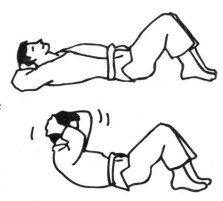

Exhale as you curl your body up and hold it a few seconds at the top. Start a situp program slowly, perhaps only ten or fifteen at a time, and progress to where you can do forty or fifty at a time. Strong abdominal muscles help keep your spine straight and thus releave back stress. You also want strong mucscles in case you are accidentaly hit in the stomach.

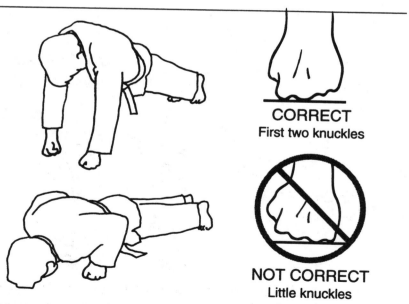

CORRECT
First two knuckles

NOT CORRECT
Little knuckles

Martial arts pushups are done with fists tight and the first two knuckles making contact with the floor. This strenghens not only the arms and shoulders but the wrists as well. It also trains you to point the knuckles for punches.

As a part of any program of physical conditioning, you should build in some endurance exercises. These activities can be as simple as walking, jogging, riding a bike, or swimming. You can also increase your cardiovascular capabilities by doing your Tae Kwon Do moves. Try performing your training patterns over and over again. Hitting a train-

ing bag with kicks and punches (bag gloves recommended) also does wonders for your endurance.

Years ago some instructors said weight training was bad for martial artists because it was thought bulky muscles would slow you down. Today, however, most teachers recommend a weight program for strength and stamina. Consult a fitness professional at a health club or spa for specific exercises for your strength training program.

BALANCES

The first Tae Kwon Do skills you must learn are stances. They are the foundation of everything else to come. Without a good stance you can't effectively punch, kick, or block.

Since no one balance will be effective in all situations, you'll learn several.

The ready stance, **chun-bi**, is the typical classroom stance. It is also the beginning and end of most forms.

The feet are parallel with the weight exactly centered. The fists are held slightly in front of the body with front knuckles pointing toward each other.

In forward or front stance, **chongul-sogi**, or **ap-sogi**, the front leg is bent and the rear leg is straight with knee locked, so your body is supported if someone pushes you from the front.

The heel of the front foot and the toe of the rear foot are at the corners of a square about one shoulder width.

The back stance, **fugil-sogi**, may not be as stable as the front stance, but it is certainly more mobile. Both legs are bent for quick motions. However most of the weight rests over the rear foot so you can quickly kick with the front leg.

Note that the heels line up on an even line. 70% of the weight is on the back foot, although you can easily shift forward and backward in this stance.

The "karate walk" is usually done in a forward stance. By sliding the foot in a slight inward direction when stepping forward, the head level will remain the same which reduces the up and down motion that can signal movement to an opponent. The center of gravity also stays even meaning that you are less likely to be caught off balance if interuppted in the middle of a step.

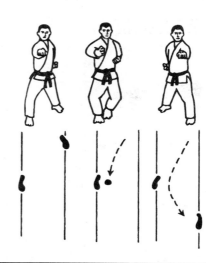

In forward stance, the about-face, **_tuiro tura_**, is done by crossing the back leg in a straight line (illustration at left). Once the distance has been established, rotate your body until you are facing the opposite direction.

In back stance (illustration at right) you merely lift your toes and pivot on your heels until you face the opposite direction. Note that the heels remain on the same line. When turning in either forward or back stance, be sure and keep the hands up so you don't turn into a punch or other attack.

41

The horse stance, **kima-sogi,** is sometimes also called a straddle stance. The feet are parallel and about one and a half to two shoulder-widths apart.

Tense the abdominal muscles and bring your hips forward to keep a straight spine and low center of gravity. Practice punching is often done in a horse stance.

The cat stance, **twitpal-sogi,** is specifically designed to allow you to kick with the front leg with little or no rocking motion to the rear. This balance resembles the back stance except that the front foot is pulled off the floor with only the ball of the foot touching.

TARGETS

Tae Kwon Do doesn't make you a superman. It just teaches you how to hit and where to hit. We'll cover the "how" in the next few pages. Here you'll find the "where." The target points can be divided into two main divisions;

1) **Primary targets**—are the points on the body where you can very easily hurt someone. These are the first areas to go to in a self-defense situation.

2) **Secondary targets**—places where it takes a little more force to hurt an attacker, but where he will still feel a well-placed strike.

It is very important to hit right on the target. You could execute a good punch or kick but if you hit him in the shoulder, for example, you will only make him mad. Your techniques are only as effective as the target they hit.

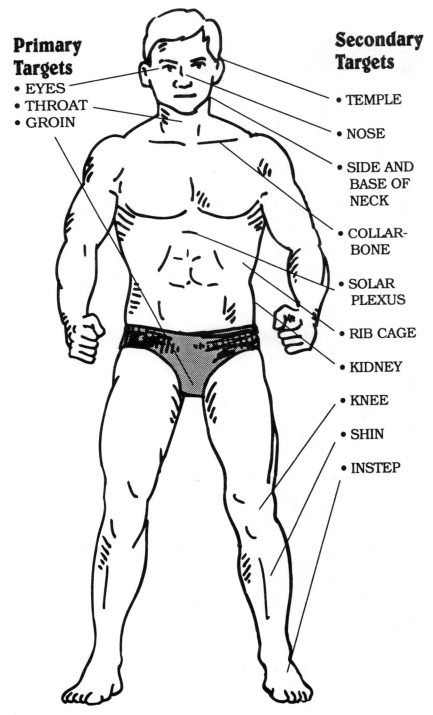

Primary Targets
- EYES
- THROAT
- GROIN

Secondary Targets
- TEMPLE
- NOSE
- SIDE AND BASE OF NECK
- COLLAR-BONE
- SOLAR PLEXUS
- RIB CAGE
- KIDNEY
- KNEE
- SHIN
- INSTEP

43

STRIKES

Empty-handed martial arts are all built on the basic premise that you can cause damage to an attacker by using your own body as a weapon. Remember, you have to hit the opponent in the right place. American Tae Kwon Do utilizes nine body parts as weapons—your hands, feet, elbows, knees, and head.

It takes diligent practice to perfect each of these blows. Positioning of the feet and the amount of body twist have as much to do with the technique's effectiveness as does muscle power and speed. Therefore you simply can't learn techniques from a book—spend time in the classroom with your instructor.

HAND TECHNIQUES

PUNCH—The most commonly used hand technique is the closed fist punch. To make a fist curl the finger tightly and tuck the thumb in.

The striking surface is the first two knuckles. Be sure and keep the wrist straight so it won't collapse on inpact.

KNIFE-HAND—Many people believe the chop is used more frequently than it really is—probably because TV and movie martial artists seem to be always using it. Wearing padded gloves in sport competition has further reduced the frequency of the knife-hand although the classic chop is still a valuable weapon for self-defense.

To form a knife-hand keep your fingers together and flex them slightly. The thumb should be bent and not extended away from the hand. As with the punch keep your wrist straight.

The striking surface is slightly to the palm side of the hand so contact with the boney edge is reduced.

The front hand punch is called a **jab**. It's a quick technique that is hard to block if you snap your hand back to the starting position. Snap also increases power in the blow which is something you need with this strike because because there is less hip motion than a reverse punch (below).

The more commonly seen **reverse punch** uses the back, or reverse, hand. This punch uses a twist of the hips to generate more power. The only drawback to this technique is that you are momentarily open for a counter-strike if you execute the reverse punch too slowly.

BODY MOVEMENT —You should use your *whole* body for a jab (or any hand strike for that matter). This gives you maximum power as well as an extended reach (see below).

Note that in all these photos the distance between the combatants' feet stays the same.

Here the attacker shoots out a jab but because he is shorter than the opponent the blow falls short.

However by simply using his body he is able to make contact with the opponent's face.
(Of course if he leans TOO far forward he'll lose his balance!)

BACKFIST—This technique hits with the back of the knuckles rather than the front surface as in a jab. It is good for a quick surprise strike because of its speed and the close proximity of the hand to the target (usually the temple or nose area). Like the jab you must snap the fist back to get the concussion effect and maximize power.

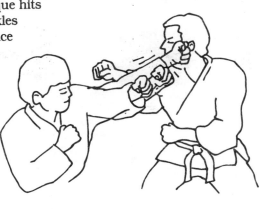

RIDGEHAND—Hit with the inside ridge of the open hand. It is especially good for striking the soft areas like the neck or throat. The angle of attack makes the ridgehand more difficult to block than a straight-line technique.

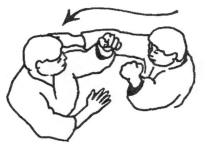

A ridgehand starts in a straight line and hooks at the last second. This final hooking motion enables the ridgehand to wrap around an opponent's block.

HAMMER FIST—Good for board breaking. Because you hit with the side of the fist instead of the knuckles (as in a punch), you are less likely to hurt your hand. Don't stop at the surface of the board but drive your hammer fist PAST the board. Don't forget to yell either!

TIGER MOUTH—Here's a good self-defense strike. The name comes from the fact that this technique resembles a tiger's open mouth.

It is especially effective in hitting the soft targets like the throat.

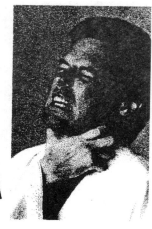

PALM HEEL—This is also a great self-defense technique. It is good for women and children who may not have large hand and knuckles. Strike with the base of the palm while pulling your fingers back out of the way.

SPLIT FINGER SPEAR—This technique is used to attack the eyes of your assailant. Obviously you would only use this if you are in danger of being hurt because you could do damage to a person's eyes if you are not careful. This is especially good for women to remember if attacked.

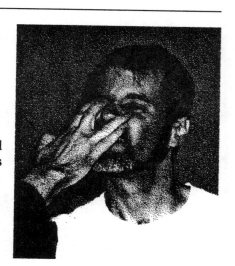

FOOT TECHNIQUES

These are the techniques that every would-be Tae Kwon Do expert imagines themselves doing. Indeed, kicks are what make Tae Kwon Do different from boxing or other kinds of fighting that use only the hands.

The leg is longer than the arm. Using kicks a smaller person can effectively hurt a larger person and still stay out of range of a punch or grab.

Your legs are not only stronger than your arms, they are longer (see the illustration). So it stands to reason that a kick is a more effective blow than a punch.

HOWEVER, the legs have several *disadvantages* in comparison to hand strikes. First, the feet are usually slower than the hands. Also, because most people don't use their legs in everyday activities like they do their arms and hands—kicks are initially awkward and take much, much more practice to execute correctly. Finally, because a fighter ends up standing on just one leg (or even none in a jumping kick), balance becomes much more critical than with a simple punch or chop.

Here are a few other points to keep in mind when attempting to kick an attacker.

1) Stay balanced. Your center of gravity must stay within your base of support. In other words if you lean too far one way or the other you'll be pushed off balance when you make contact.

2) Keep your eyes on your opponent. If you look away as you kick, you're likely to miss (this is a common mistake with beginners).

3) Don't just use the weight of your leg, move your whole body and hips into the kick. This increases momentum and puts everything you've got behind it.

4) Snap the foot back immediately to keep it from being grabbed.

5) Your fold should not give away your imminent attack. That means don't swing or lift your arms before you kick. Don't lean over or twist your body until the kick is on its way. If you raise your arms and lean back before you even start to kick I can guarantee your opponent will be able to avoid or block it.

6) Keep your hands up when you kick. After all, the reason you are kicking your opponent in the first place is, HE IS TRYING TO HIT YOU! It would be foolish to keep your hands at your side when some one is attempting to break your nose.

ap-chagi
FRONT KICK

Start by raising the kicking foot up to knee level.

Snap the foot out striking with the ball of the foot. Note the slight thrust forward with the hips to gain distance and power.

Immediately snap the foot back to the knee.

yop-chagi
SIDE KICK

Raise the kicking foot up to knee level.

Snap the foot out striking with the heel of the foot. (A Okinawan karate style side kick usually hits with the blade of the foot.)

Immediately snap the foot back to the knee.

tolyo-chagi
ROUND HOUSE KICK

Twist the body bringing the kicking leg up high and point the knee towards your target.

Snap the kick out striking with either the ball of the foot (shown) or the instep.

Immediately snap the foot back keeping the knee up.

51

BACK KICK

With your back toward the opponent, fold the kicking leg up to the knee.

Looking over your shoulder, snap the kick out striking with the heel. Be sure to bring the kick back.

HOOKING HEEL KICK

As the name implies, this kick hooks back into the target, striking with the back of your heel.

CRESCENT KICK

The crescent kick begins like a front kick with the knee raised high.

The striking surface is the inside bottom edge of the foot. This is the kick often used to knock something out of an attacker's hand.

TURNING BACK KICK

Turn your back toward the opponent. You might want to fake a backfist or other hand technique to cover your turn-around.

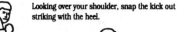

Looking over your shoulder, snap the kick out striking with the heel.

Be sure to snap the foot back so your opponent cannot grab your leg.

DOUBLE JUMP FRONT KICK

Begin by executing a normal front snap kick.

As you bring the kick back leap off the ground with the opposite foot.

Jump forward with the second kick.

BLOCKING

While your best defense is, of course, avoiding a fight in the first place, sometimes you have to defend yourself with blocking techniques. Because most Karate and Tae Kwon Do schools are hard-style "striking" arts, most of the blocks are, in essense, defensive *strikes* used to stop or deflect an attacker's blows. When executing offensive strikes many parts of your body can be used to perform the techniques. Below are the first five of the many possible blocks. Not all schools have these exact hand positions, but they are similar.

A **low block,**
hardan-marki,
is used to defend from
a strike to the abdomen
or groin.

Begin by crossing the
blocking arm on top. Step out
into a forward stance while
forcefully dropping the fist.
The contact point is the
forearm. Pull the opposite
hand back to increase body
twist and power.

A **rising block,**
chukyo-marki,
deflects a downward
strike.

Raise the non-blocking arm
and lower the other fist in front
of the groin to protect that
area. Step out in a forward
stance and swing the forearm
up. The fist should be high
over the head to deflect the
attack.

A **outside-inside block,**
ahn-marki or some-
times also called
arb-cheegi,
defends the
face area.

Pull the blocking arm behind
your head. Step out in a
forward stance and block with
the inner forearm. Just before
impact rotate the wrist so the
palm turns toward your face.

AMERICAN TAE KWON DO

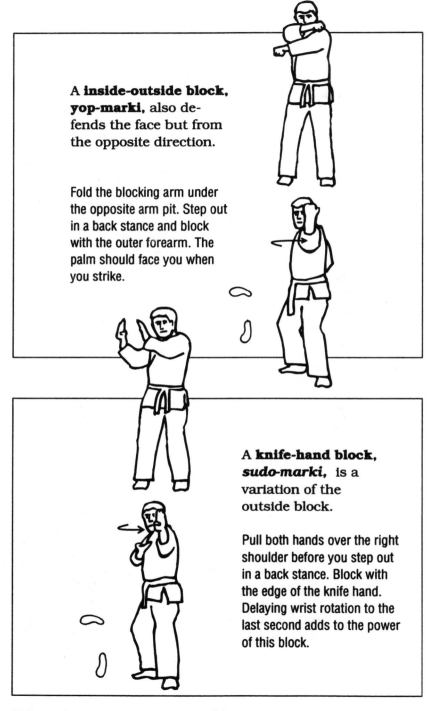

A **inside-outside block, yop-marki,** also defends the face but from the opposite direction.

Fold the blocking arm under the opposite arm pit. Step out in a back stance and block with the outer forearm. The palm should face you when you strike.

A **knife-hand block, sudo-marki,** is a variation of the outside block.

Pull both hands over the right shoulder before you step out in a back stance. Block with the edge of the knife hand. Delaying wrist rotation to the last second adds to the power of this block.

Ahop Palchuk Marki
Nine-Step Block

The Nine-Step Block Pattern is used in American Tae Kwon Do
Nam Seo Kwan as a simple way to learn the basic blocking techniques.

Yell

Chunbi   1.   2.   3.

4.   5. Turn   6.

7.   8.   9. Turn   Go-mon   Shio

57

To hear is to forget,
To see is to remember,
To do is to understand.
Chinese Proverb

CHAPTER FIVE
FORMS

Training patterns were developed as a way to practice stances, blocks, strikes, focus, and power. Breathing, flow of technique and concentration are all important. Different styles of Karate and Tae Kwon Do use different patterns but the purpose remains the same.

Each belt advancement requires that you learn one or two new forms (or **hyung** in Korean). Usually the beginning forms are simple with only a handful of different movements. The higher you go the harder the forms become.

HISTORY

The Shaolin monks were the first to practice training routines. As the Chinese influence spread throughout Asia, martial arts forms spread also.

Since modern Tae Kwon Do came from a combination of native Korean systems plus Okinawan and Japanese influences, many of the first Tae Kwon Do forms in the 1940s and 50s were just like Karate **kata**.

General Choi Hong Hi created new forms soon after the birth of Tae Kwon Do in 1955. He had trained in Shotokan Karate and so his forms had much the same emphasis relying, for example, on low stances and direct, powerful kicks. These were the **Chang-Hon** (or Blue Cottage) patterns, sometimes refered to as the **Chunji** patterns, after the name of the first form.

These were the forms first learned by Nam Seo Kwan's founder, Mr. Yates, and thus are the foundation of Tae Kwon Do Nam

Seo Kwan's required patterns. The **first four forms** are demonstrated on the following pages.

PERFORMANCE HINTS

There are several things you can do to make your forms not only look better but actually serve their orginal purpose more effectively—that is, to help you develop your techniques.

1) Do each strike and block as if you were using it for real. Imagine a real opponent.

2) At the begining stages a student is often told to step first and then execute the technique. At the advanced stages you should learn how to step and strike together. Developing this sense of timing gives you a rythym.

3) Think "economy of motion." Don't make unecessary motions; make every move count for something.

4) Contol your breathing—exhaling on each step, and sometimes even on a preparation for a step.

5) Be aware of your balance and stances. Footwork is just as important as where you put your hands.

THE FORMS OF
AMERICAN TAE KWON DO NAM SEO KWAN

CHUNJI .... Orange Belt
TANGUN .... Purple Belt
TOE SAN .... Green Belt
WON HYO .... Blue Belt
YUL GOOK .... 3rd Brown
CHUNG GUEN ...... 3rd Brown
TIE GIE .... 2nd Brown
HWA RANG .... 2nd Brown
CHUG MU .... 1st Brown
CHUL GI .... 1st Brown

KWANG GYE .... 1st Black
BASAI.................... 1st Black
SIP SOO .... 2nd Black
PO UN .... 2nd Black
KAE BEK .... 3rd Black
CHOI YOUNG .... 4th Black
NAM SEO HYUNG 4th Black

CHUNJI

The name means "Heaven and Earth," a fitting name for the very first form. This form has 19 steps.

Note that EXTENDED arm folds on TOP (the "heaven" side).

YELL signals end of first half.

NOTE: This form is done in a pattern shaped like a "cross."

continued on next page

AMERICAN TAE KWON DO

Note on second half of form the EXTENDED hand folds on bottom (the "earth" side).

YELL on last step

On "Goman" command step up to Ready Position

APPLICATION OF MOVEMENTS

It is very important that you understand the movements of each form. There isn't space to explain every step so we'll just demonstrate a few of the movements so you can visualize the block or strike. Ask your instructor if you do not understand a certain move.

CHUNJI actually has only two combinations. Above is the low block and counter punch from the first half of the form (at the advanced stages you will learn more complicated applications for these basic moves).

This is the outside block and counter punch from the second half of the pattern.

TANGUN

Named after the legendary founder of Korea.

YELL

YELL

65

APPLICATION

The box block is introduced in Tangun form (steps no. 9
and 11) and will be used in other patterns. It indicates a
defense against a double attack from two different
opponents.

Tangun also introduces the idea of a multiple block (step
no. 13). The attack is a low kick and high hammer fist.
The down block and rising block are performed quickly.

TOESAN

Pseudonym of the great Korean patriot, Ahn Chang Ho (1876–1938).

YELL

1

2 3 4 5 6

7 8

AMERICAN TAE KWON DO

YELL

The first step of Toe San is a hammer fist —outside block followed by a middle punch.

This sequence consists of a double outside knife-hand block followed by chops to the collarbone . . .

. . . then grab the opponent and execute a front kick and two middle punches.

WON HYO

Named after the monk who introduced Buddhism to the Silla Dynasty in ancient Korea.

YELL!

1

2

3   **4**   **5**   **6**

7

8

9

YELL!

10

11

12

13 Gomon

TO KNOW
AND TO ACT
ARE ONE
AND THE SAME.
Samurai
Axiom

CHAPTER SIX
SPARRING

Although forms teach you the principles of effective fighting, they cannot by themselves prepare you for combat against an actual opponent. Things like timed response to an attack and the feel of a block against a real strike aimed at your face are vital preparation for a real fight. So Karate, Tae Kwon Do, and other combat-oriented martial arts incorporate mock-fights or sparring into their training.

Because of the possibility of injury, most schools don't let white belts spar. Some dojangs wait until students reach the third or fourth belt level before introducing sparring.

In spite of the fact that the participants are throwing kicks and punches at each other, sparring is really pretty safe. Padded hand and foot pads as well as a mouthpiece and helmet are recommended. Boys should wear a protective groin cup.

EMPHASIS

Sparring varies from art to art and even from school to school within the same martial art system. In some classes the teachers put great emphasis on "sport" sparring. Instruction focuses on tournament rules and on how to score points. Other teachers stress a more realistic type of sparring where "anything goes." Probably the best approach is a balanced one. Rules are necessary, especially for beginning level students, but a knowledge of realistic techniques is also needed to prepare the student for actual street fights.

ONE-STEP SPARRING

The safest transitional step between forms and all-out sparring (often also called freestyle) is prearranged sparring drills commonly called "one-step" sparring, *il-bo taeryon*. The first one-steps you will learn are fairly simple, but they get harder as you move up the ranks. The basic six one-steps used in American Tae Kwon Do Nam Seo Kwan are illustrated on the following pages. After you learn these six you will get to create your own original one-steps for advanced-belt promotions.

ONE-STEP ATTACK SEQUENCE

The defender yells (1), giving the signal that he or she is ready for the attack.

The attacker steps back with the **right** foot and executes a down block with a loud yell (2).

Then the attacker steps forward with a **right** punch to the defender's face while the defender performs the block and counter attack (3) After completing the sequence both partners return to ready position (4).

The one-step routine continues with the defender yelling once again and the attacker steping back, blocking and attacking, this time with the **left** punch.

Then the roles change as the defender becomes the attacker. The other person must now demonstrate a pair of one-step sparring sequences.

1–Drop into a back balance (your lead foot is the same as the attacker's lead foot–a closed stance) and do a inside block.

2–Backfist to the face area. The initial block and backfist should be done very quickly.

3–Finish with a reverse punch to the solar plexus.

2

1–Knife
hand
outside
block.

2–Reverse
punch to the
solar plexus.

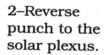

3–Rising
plam heel
to the face.

3

1–Drop into a back balance (this time in a open stance) and do a outside knife-hand block.

2–Execute a front snap kick to opponent's groin.

3–4–After putting the kicking leg down do two punches to the attacker's mid-section.

4

1–Ready for the attack.

2–Step to the outside of the attack and execute an outside scooping block with a knife-hand.

3–Do a round kick to the attacker's mid-section while grabbing the wrist.

4–Finish with a reverse punch to the ribs.

5

1–Step to the outside and perform a "T block."

2–Grab with your top hand and pull the opponent into a chop to the ribs.

3–With the same hand execute a chop to the neck.

4–Finish with a knee to the abdomen using the back leg.

1–Perform an out
  side block while
  striking the
  throat with a tiger
  mouth.

2–Chop to the collarbone.

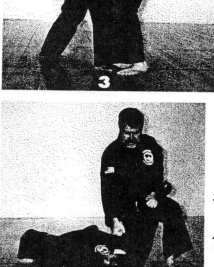

3–Grabbling both hands,
  swing your back leg up.

4–Execute a take-down by
  hitting your calf muscle
  against the attacker's calf.

5–Finish with a punch or a
  stomp.

FREESTYLE SPARRING

Even the fanciest one-steps are a far cry from freestyle sparring which is as close to an actual street fight as you can get without running the risk of great injury or even death (always a possibilty in a real fight).

One of the biggest mistakes beginners make is not following up an initial attack with another technique. In fact, one reason we practice one-steps is to learn multiple techniques. Here are a few basic combinations.

BLOCK AND COUNTER COMBINATION
Moving inside a hooking heel kick to execute a punch to the body.

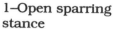

1–Open sparring stance

2–Cross over with your back foot and at the same time strike with the front back-fist. This draws the opponent's attention away from your step.

3–Grab the sleeve with the front hand and fold high with the kicking leg.

4–Side thrust kick.

Multiple-kick combination

1–Open sparring stance

2–Low round kick...

3–Followed by a quick face kick.

4–Set the foot down and turn your body.

5–Finish with a turning back kick.

WHAT ABOUT TOURNAMENTS?

Although there were some small competitions held in the early sixties, national tournaments really started in 1964 with the first National Championships put on in Washington D.C. by Jhoon Rhee and the Long Beach Internationals sponsored by Ed Parker the same year. So-called world and national tournaments have been sprouting up all across America ever since.

The term "so-called" is appropriate here because the vast majority of tournaments were and still are regional events in spite of names like "United States," "American," "World," etc. in their titles.

In 1973 foam-rubber sparring gear was introduced by Jhoon Rhee which changed the face of competition forever. Also around this time semi-contact was officially introduced (although it had be unofficially practiced for years) and prize money was first offered.

But by the late seventies the highly visible competition scene faded, both because of a martial arts business slump and because of a lack of support from the martial arts media. With less prestige available and with less money to spend, competitors traveled less and there were practically no real national tournaments anymore.

Today that situation is still largely the same although there are several national ratings organizations that have tried to establish criteria for "national" tournaments with varying degrees of success. Of course, the bottom line is, unless you are a champion-caliber black belt competitor, you shouldn't really be concerned with the "rating" of a tournament. You should only want to compete in order to challenge yourself and to test your abilities against someone at the same level of development.

Why Some Schools Don't Do Tournaments At All

It seems like most Karate and Tae Kwon Do schools have dozens of trophies in their front windows, implying that their students are tournament champions. The fact of the matter is there is a surprisingly large minority of martial arts schools that don't participate in tournaments at all.

Their reasons vary. Critics of these "non-competition" schools say they don't want to be shown to have inferior styles. That may be true in isolated cases, but most actually have some valid arguments against tournaments.

Some teachers don't like the attitude often displayed in open events. Indeed, if you aren't careful, you can learn bad habits like arguing with the officials, yelling for someone to "kill" someone else (a common problem for some parents), and blaming others for your own lack of skills. For these reasons some instructors won't allow their students to participate in any tournaments.

Other schools have "closed events"—that is only competitors of a single school or organization may participate in order to control the atmosphere and the enforcement of rules.

Another reason for not participating in tournaments is that tournaments are considered "play" martial arts rather than "real" martial arts. These instructors say that martial arts can only be fully practiced in a life or death manner and that competing for points dilutes the techniques to the point of impracticality.

How to Score Tournament Points

This is going to be a very brief explaination of tournament scoring. That's not because scoring a point in a competition isn't very complicated. In fact, it can be pretty confusing.

The reason is different parts of the country have different rules and regulations. Sometimes you will even find different rules in the same city, depending on the organization sponsoring the tournament. As a result, we will have to be fairly general in our discussion.

Points are scored when you throw a good technique to a regulation target area. A majority of the judges must agree that you scored. At the end of the time limit (usually two minutes) the person with the most points wins.

Pointers on Scoring

The jab at the left is too far away. The judges want you to get within two or three inches in order to score a point.

At right is a jab right on target. In most tournaments adult brown and black belts are allowed light face touch. Children generally cannot hit their opponent in the face or they will give up a point.

At the left you can see how the kicker is leaning too far backward to have any effective power. No point(s) would be awarded.

At right the kick to the head is executed with better balance. At many American tournaments a head kick is worth two points instead of one because of the degree of difficulty. Check the rules for your event.

Successful sparring is an art. It takes long hours of practice to become good at it. Some students are natural atheletes and excell quickly while others take months, perhaps years to become competant. This is probably the one area of martial arts practice that causes more students to quit training than any other.

It is easy to become discouraged with your sparring. Study some of the principles of effective sparring and try to practice them.

BODY POSITION—This is a very important principle. The position of your body determines not only what techniques you can hit your opponent with but also what he can hit you with.

He who fears being conquered is sure of defeat.
—Napolean Bonaparte

DISTANCE—You want to control the distance rather than letting your opponent control it. If you are a good kicker then you can spar from a somewhat greater distance. If, on the other hand, your opponent is the better kicker, you don't want to position yourself where he can easily kick you and you have to try and close the gap in order to punch him effectively. You must become a master at controling the distance if you want to be an effective fighter.

SPEED—This is one of the two elements of power, the other being body mass. Although most people realize they can increase their body mass through strength exercises they often don't think about also increasing their speed. According to Ed Parker, the "father" of American karate, there are three types of speed.

—Perceptual: How quickly you recognize external stimuli. This would be, for example, your ability to sense trouble. Another word for it might be awareness.

—Mental: How quickly you react to the stimuli. You must know the techniques well enough that they are instinctive. The more you know the faster you can respond.

—Physical: How quickly your body moves. Several factors come into play here. Your fitness level, your limberness and your efficiency of movement are all important.

Finally, you should realize that tournament sparring, however good it may be for self-confidence and for working on your speed, focus, etc. is not an *exact* preparation for a street-fight. It is very different to face an opponent when there are no rules and when there is no referee to call "break."

Be Prepared!

Not every tiger will pounce,
but every tiger may pounce.

Old Karate Axiom

CHAPTER SEVEN
SELF-DEFENSE

Self-defense is the main reason most people take Karate or Tae Kwon Do. Most instructors will tell you that you aren't going to be able to defend your-self effectively with martial arts until at least ten or twelve months into your practice. The reason is simple—fights seldom go as planned. There are too many variables to be able to say that a certain defense from a certain attack is going to work every time. You have to know more than just a few basic techniques to prepare for the dangerous possibilities of a real self-defense situation.

Some instructors place too much emphasis on what to do *after* you get into a confrontation rather than on how to avoid a confrontation in the first place. You have heard about "street-smarts'" and the important role that plays in self-protection. Much of self-defense, just like much of sparring, is mental rather than physical. You must use common sense to avoid a confrontation.

P-R-E FIGHT

Memorize this. It is what you want to do BEFORE you have to use your Tae Kwon Do in a fight.

"P" stands for **prevention**: Do what you can to avoid any kind of confrontation. Set up rules ahead of time–don't talk to strangers, park under a streetlight if you won't be returning to your car until after dark, ask for ID if someone comes to your door, etc.

"R" is for **recognition**: Be aware of your surroundings so you are less likely to be caught in a bad situation. Look into your car before you get in. Notice if someone is following you or even just staring at you. Pay attention to things around you!

"E" stands for **escape**: Run away from a possible fight. Even experienced black belts will back down before they have to use their martial arts—you should too!

Finally—only as a last resort—**fight** to protect your-self and your loved ones. If it comes to this point don't hesitate. Use your best techniques and do it quickly and effectively.

89   AMERICAN TAE KWON DO

In American Tae Kwon Do Nam Seo Kwan we require pre-set self-defense routines for the first few beginners' ranks, but by purple belt the student should be able to execute self-defense technqiues in a "freestyle" manner.

Remember that every opponent is different and every situation is different. Therefore in order to be truly effective you must be able to do these freestyle self-defense moves without having to stop and think.

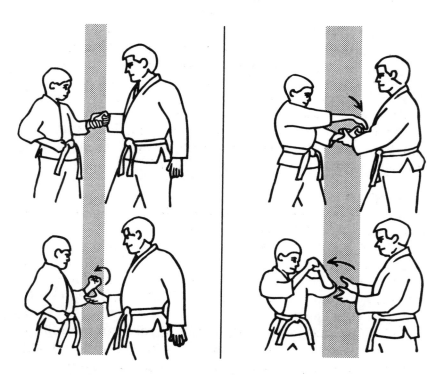

SIMPLE WRIST GRAB—In order to escape from a stronger opponent you must twist your wrist AGAINST his thumb. The theory is that your entire arm should be stronger than his thumb. Sometimes, however, the attacker's thumb IS as strong as the victim's arm (a strong man against a child or small woman, for example). In this case you should use TWO hands to escape. This also works when the attacker uses two hands to grab your wrist.

FRONT CHOKE ESCAPE—Reach over and through the attacker's arms and clasp your hands together. Twist your shoulders and hips toward your top hand (in this case the defender's left arm is on top so he twists to the left).

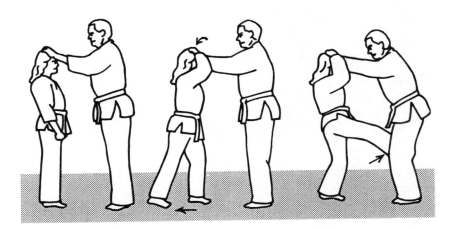

HAIR PULL—Immediately pull the attacker's hand tight to your head so he can't pull your hair. Step back to prepare for a kick and then strike to the groin with your instep.

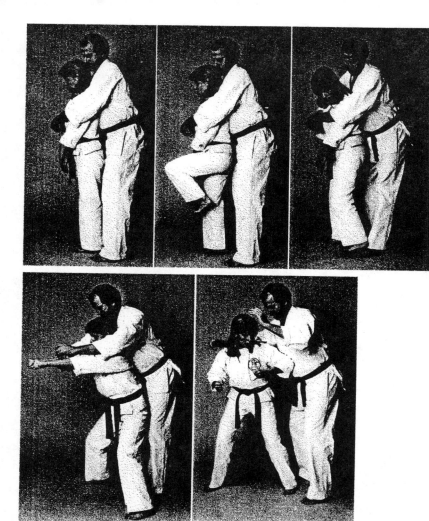

REAR BEAR HUG

Stomp on the attacker's instep with your heel. This weakens his grip enabling you to drop and extend your arms. Twist into an elbow strike to his solar plexus. Don't forget to run away after you have weakened him with your elbow.

REAR FOREARM CHOKE

Your first priority is to prevent the attack from cutting off your air. Grab his forearm and pull forward until you can tuck your chin behind his arm to relieve pressure on your throat.

Now stomp on his instep. Immediately follow up with an elbow strike to his stomach or solar plexus. You can finish him off with a low knife-hand chop to the groin.

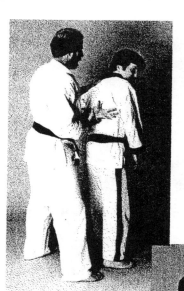

HAMMER LOCK

Do not turn into or towards the grab (a strong opponent could break your arm) but instead twist around hitting the attacker with an elbow strike to the head.

If he leans out of the way, you can simply continue your turning motion and hit with a knife-hand.

FULL NELSON

Clasp your hands together and press back against your own forehead. This releaves the pressure of the attack. If he is strong you won't be able to hold him off for very long . . . so quickly execute a rising heel to his groin.

You can now reach up, grab a finger and pull the attacker's hand away. If he resists simply break the finger. A twisting elbow stike finishes him off.

HEAD LOCK

Reach up behind the attacker's head to grab a hand-full of his hair. Yank back and strike with your opposite hand.

OTHER EVERYDAY WEAPONS

You probably have at your disposal several weapons and never even realized it. For exmple, car keys are a very effective tool for self-defense. Hold them in the manner shown between your index finger and thumb. This is the most secure way to hold a key for strikes and slashes at an attacker's face. Needless to say, you can cause permanent damage like blindness when using a sliver of metal to someone's face. However if it is his life or yours, We suggest that yours is more important to you.

Other common items that can be used in self-defense are pens, pencils, combs, sticks, and rocks. Be creative in the use of your surroundings.

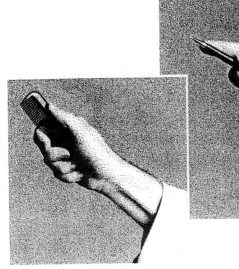

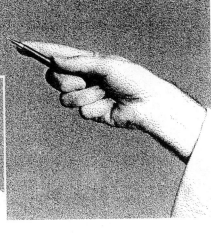

97

*"The student is in the dojo
to become like the teacher, to acquire not
just the teacher's technical skills but
something of his attitude and character,
much as a son grows to resemble his father."*

Chuck Norris

*Karate champion and movie star
Chuck Norris with author Keith Yates.*

CHAPTER NINE
GLOSSARY

Here are some of the terms you might hear in an American Tae Kwon Do class. I will not list terms I have already mentioned in previous chapters, such as the names of certain techniques. When there is a Japanese equivalent that is frequently used I have also listed that wording. There are several other terms listed here that I think an American stylist should know. —*KDY*

AMERICAN KARATE An eclectic blend of traditional Asian forms of Karate-like arts. While such an integration of philosophies and techniques is not unique to the United States, Americans have popularized this approach during the last half of the 20th century. Korean-based stylists often use the term "American Tae Kwon Do."

BODHIDHARMA (Bowd´-hid-har-mah) Indian. The monk who supposedly went to the Shaolin Monestary around 525 AD and formulated a series of exercises that evolved into Temple Boxing or Kung Fu.

BUDO (boo´-doh) Japan. "way of fighting." A generic term refering to the contemporary Japanese martial arts which have more of a psychological emphasis than the older warrior arts known as Bujutsu.

BUSHIDO (boo-she´-doh) Japan. "way of the warrior." The code of behavior of the Samurai, first formulated during the peaceful times of the Tokugawa Shogunate (1603–1886). It placed great stress on duty and loyalty to the Samurai's lord.

CENTERING A concept found in all martial arts refering to a calmness and balance of mental and emotional energies. If you are centered, you are relaxed and yet alert. The "center" of the body is a point about two inches below the navel.

CHANG-HON (chang´-hawn) Korea. "blue cottage" The pen name of General Choi Hong Hi and the name used to refer to the training patterns he designed around traditional karate forms.

CHOONGDAN (choong´-dan) Kor. "middle" or "center."

DAERYON (daw´-ryon) Korea. "sparring." The Japanese term is "kumite."

DAN (dawn) Japan./Korea. "step" or "degree." Term used for black belt rank holders. First degree black belt is often called the first step to a higher level of learning.

DANJUN (dawn-jun´) Korea. Area just below navel which is the center of gravity and believed to also be center of energy. Japanese is "hara."

DARUMA (dar´-ma) Japanese name for BODHIDHARMA.

DO (dough) Japan. "way" or "path." Refers to a disciplined approach to the martial arts to achieve personal development.

DOJANG (dough´-jang) Korea. "the place of the way" The training hall or gymnasium. "Dojo" in Japanese. Chinese is "kwoon."

GOMAN (go-mawn) Korea. "end." Japanese is "Ma te."

GUP (gup) Kor. "grade." Term for ranks below black belt. Japanese term is "kyu."

HARD STYLES These approaches rely primarily on force-against-force rather than the yielding movements of soft styles. Hard martial arts (which often contain soft elements as well) are typified by Karate and Tae Kwon Do. Sometimes refered to as "external" styles.

HARDAN (har´-dan) Kor. "low level."

HOSIN SUL (hoh´-sin sool) Korea. "self-defense techniques."

HWA RANG-DO (wa-rang´-dough) Korea. "way of the flower of manhood." Code of behavior of the ancient hwa-rang warriors of Korea. Similar to the Japanese Bushido, code of the Samurai. Also a modern Korean martial art style.

HYUNG/KATA

HYUNG (hyoung) Kor. "form." Japanese word is "kata." Prearranged patterns and movements used in training. The word "poomse" is used for forms in the World Tae Kwon Do Federation.

ILBO TAERYON (eyell´-bo tay´-ryon) Korea. "One-step sparring." A method of training in which your partner attacks with a single step, allowing you to practice your block and counter attack. Used in most martial systems. Japanese is "Ippon Kumite."

JANG KWAN NIM (jang´-kwan nim) Korea. "honored headmaster." Refers to the founder of a kwan (school).

JUDO (joo´-dough) Japan. Usually translated "gentle way." Founded in 1882 by Jigoro Kano, a ju jutsu master. Based on overcoming an opponents attack by using his strength against him by twisting and turning your body. Utilizes many sweeps and throws. The atemi-waza (striking techniques) are used only for self-defense and not in competition. Judo was the first martial art to be recognized as an Olympic sport in 1960.

JU-JUTSU (joo-jut´-soo) Japan. "art of flexibility," or "art of suppleness" or "art of
gentleness." Unlike its softer offspring
judo, jujutsu utilizes a lot of striking and
blocking in its arsenal of throws, chokes,
and joint-locks.

JU-JUTSU

KARA (ka´-ra) "empty" or "china." Japanese
pronunciation of either of two ideograms
pared with "te" to create Karate.
Originally "kara" (china hand) was used
but Gichin Funakoshi reportedly
changed the word to "empty hand."

KARATE (ka´-ra-tay) Japan. "empty hand."

KATA (ka´-ta) Japan. "formal exercise."
Korean is "hyung."

KI (kee) Korea. / Japan. "spirit," "breath," "vital energy." Energy created from
a combination of proper breathing, mental concentration, and physical
technique. Known as "Chi" in Chinese martial arts.

KIAP (kee´-ahp) Japan. "spirit meeting." The yell of the martial as fist which is
supposed to concentrate the physical, mental, and spiritual
energies all together. "Kia" in Japanese.

KUKKIWON (kuk´-kee-wan) Korea. The headquarters of Korean style TKD
located in Seoul, South Korea.

KUNG FU (kong foo´) Chin. "skill," "strength," "task." Literally means a
strength or skill to do a certain task. Has
come to be a generic term to designate the
Chinese martial arts.

NINJA

MARKI (mar´-key) Korea. "block." Also translated as
MAKGI (maw´-ghee).

NINJA (nin´-jah) Japan. "stealer in" or "spy." Hired
assassins, terrorists, and spies in feudal
Japan. Unlike the Samurai, they had no
allegiance to anyone. They became legends in
the 13th to 17th centuries in Japan because
of their reputed skills of stealth.

PARRO (pah´-row) Korea. "return." Often used in
Korean martial arts classes as a command to
resume the ready posture.

101

POOMSE (poom´-say) See Hyung

PRESSURE POINTS Specific vital areas of the body which, when struck with minimal force, create maximum pain. The art and science of pressure points can be used for health (acupressure and acupuncture) or to cause death (see dim mak).

SABUM (sah´-bim) Korea. "instructor." Korean equivalent to Japanese "Sensei." Sometimes the suffix "nim" is added as in SABUM-NIM to indicate added respect.

SAMURAI (som´-uh-reye) Japan. "warrior" or "one who serves." Feudal Japanese warriors who served their lords. Codes of conduct were established for both lords and their samurai after 1600 during the Tokugawa shogunate era.

SANGDAN (sang´-dan) Korea. "upper level." Japan. is "jodan."

SENSEI (sehn´-say) Japan. "teacher" or, more literally "old one." Has come to refer to an instructor in Japanese and Okinawan martial arts. Korean equivalent is "sabum." Chinese is "sifu."

SHAOLIN (sha´-oh-lin) The Chinese temple where Bodhidharma taught his 18 exercises to the monks. Actually there is more than one Shaolin Temple. Today there are several styles of "Shaolin Kung Fu" each claiming a direct link to Bodhidharma. Shaolin styles tend to be among the "harder" styles of Kung Fu.

SHIO (sheeoh) Korea. "at ease."

SHEJAK (shee´-jok) Korea. "begin." Japanese is "hajime."

SIMSA (sim´-sah) Korea. "rank testing."

SOFT STYLES These approaches to the martial arts tend to feature yielding and "blending" movements rather than the forceful blocks and strikes of the hard styles. Sometimes also called "internal styles" because of their emphasis on "inner power." Examples would be Japanese Aikido and Chinese Tai Chi.

TAE KYON (teye´-kyun) Korea. An ancient Korean fighting art.

TAE KWON DO (teye´-kwon-dough) Korea. "kick punch way."

WHICH STYLE IS BEST?

Every art has its strengths and weaknesses.

TAI CHI CHUAN (tie´-chee-chwan) Chin. One of the major internal styles of Kung Fu. Its slow, natural movements have made it a popular method of physical fitness in China.

TANG SOO DO (tang´-soo-dough) Korea. "China hand way" Korean translation of "Karate" and one of the original martial arts brought to America in the 1950s.

TI (tee) Korea. "belt." Japanese is "obi."

TOBOK (dough-bawk) Korea. "uniform." Japanese name is "gi."

WU SHU (woo´-shoo) Chi. "national sport." The official mainland name for Chinese boxing. There are two main divisions: hard styles (Shaolin) and soft styles (tai-chi, pa-kua, hsing-i).

YANG (yang) Chin. "active / positive." One side of the concept of equal opposites.

YIN (yin) Chin. "passive / negative."

Teaching a child that he can accomplish a difficult goal is to teach him success in life.

Keith D. Yates

KOREAN COUNTING

One — Hana
Two — Dul
Three — Set
Four — Net
Five — Ta sot
Six — Ya sot
Seven — Ilgup
Eight — Yudol
Nine — Ahope
Ten — Yul
Eleven — Yul Hana
Twenty — Sumul
Twenty One — Sumul Hana
Thirty — Sorum
Thirty One — Sorum Hana

First — Il, Cho
Second — Yi
Third — SaM
Fourth — Sah
Five — Oh
Sixth — Yuk
Seventh — Chil
Eight — Pal
Ninth — Koo
Tenth — Sip

Since 1976
MIND
HEART
BODY

**American Karate
and Tae Kwon Do
Organization**

MEMBERSHIP INFORMATION

You have already read about the A-KaTo in the pages of this book. We are not the biggest organization around but we are one of the best. Here's why. We won't accept just anyone with twenty dollars and the ability to fill out a form (believe it or not, some black belts have gotten their credentials just that way).

ALL of our instructors have either earned their black belts under the rigorous standards of the A-KaTo or they have been recommended for membership personally by one of our other senior instructors.

If you are an individual student studying with a school that is NOT an A-KaTo member school, sorry but we cannot sign you up as a member. If your school is not affiliated with another organization you might want to talk to your instructor because we'll be happy to send out more information about our requirements.

Actually our requirements are pretty simple. You must be a quality-minded, legitimate martial artist. For membership in Mr. Yates' Tae Kwon Do *Nam Seo Kwan* style there are more things that he will want to know about your school. However you can join the A-KaTo without becoming a part of Nam Seo Kwan.

American Karate and Tae Kwon Do Organization
1218 Cardgian Street
Garland, TX 75040

A-KaTo MEMBERSHIP APPLICATION

Since 1976

MIND
HEART
BODY

Student Members: You must belong to an A-KaTo member school to
become an individual student member.
Instructor Member: You must first be recommended by a current
A-KaTo senior instructor.

IF YOU DON'T WANT TO CUT UP YOUR BOOK, JUST PHOTOCOPY THIS PAGE.

name_____ age_____

address_____

city, state, zip_____

home phone (   ) _____ rank_____

How long in karate?_____ Instructor(s)_____

If training more than one year give a brief history of you martial arts background.

If this is an Instructor Application please list your recommending A-KaTo Instructor (3rd dan or higher)
along with their address (so we can verify your application).

_____

☐ **This is my first year's STUDENT dues — $20**
I will receive a <u>Patch</u>, New Member's <u>Manual</u>, and a Membership <u>Card</u>. In addition I will pick up
my quarterly *Sidekick Jr. Newspaper* from my instructor. I understand I will also be eligible to
attend A-KaTo examinations, tournaments, special seminars and classes.

☐ **This a BLACK BELT Membership — $25 per year**   A FREE Black Belt Membership is
given for each ten student members. First time black belts will receive an A-KaTo <u>Instructor's</u>
<u>Manual</u> and an <u>instructor's patch</u> to go under the A-KaTo patch. Black Belts will also have the
special Instructor's only newsletter, the *Sensei,* mailed directly to their address listed above.
Special Instructor's only classes will also be scheduled throughout the year.

I promise to uphold the standards of the AKaTo and to be a responsible member.

Signed_____ Date_____

INDEX

A-KaTo
  Application 105
  History of 13–15
American TKD 13
Balances 40–42
Belts 27–29
Blocking 54–57
Bodhidharma 6, 7
Bowing 21, 27
Choi, Hong Hi 8
Chunji 61–63
Counting 103
Dojang 30
Endurance 39
Foot Techniques 49–53
Forms, History of.... 59–60
Funakoshi, Gichin 7, 8
Hand Techniques ... 44–48
Havanas, Demetrius 12
Hwa Rang...................... 8
Japan........................ 7, 8
Kano, Jigoro 27
Karate 8
Korea 8
Korean Karate 11
Kung Fu 7
Kwan.............................. 8
Lee, Bruce 20
Mullins, Skipper 12
Nam Seo Kwan 14
Norris, Chuck.............. 12
Okinawa........................ 7
Olympic TKD 9
Push Ups 38
Rhee, Jhoon 10, 11, 17

Rules of the Classroom 32
Shaolin Monastery 7
Sit Ups 38
Sparring
  Freestyle 81
  One Step 73–80
Steen, Allen 10, 11, 15
Stretching 35–37
Student Pledge 22
Subak 8
Tae Kwon Do 8
Taekyon 8
Tang Soo Do 8
Tangun 64–66
Targets 42–43
Tenents of TKD............ 18
Texas Karate 10
Toe San 67–69
Tournaments.......... 84–87
Uniform..................... 27
Warm Ups 35
Weight Lifting 39
Won Hyo 70–71
Yates, Keith................. 13
Yin Yang...................... 23

If you lose . . .
Don't lose the
lesson as well!